MznLnx

Missing Links Exam Preps

Exam Prep for

Selling ASAP

Jones, Stevens, & Chonko, 1st Edition

The MznLnx Exam Prep is your link from the texbook and lecture to your exams.
The MznLnx Exam Preps are unauthorized and comprehensive reviews of your textbooks.

MznLnx

Rico
Publications

Exam Prep for Selling ASAP
1st Edition
Jones, Stevens, & Chonko

Publisher: Raymond Houge
Assistant Editor: Michael Rouger
Text and Cover Designer: Lisa Buckner
Marketing Manager: Sara Swagger
Project Manager, Editorial Production: Jerry Emerson
Art Director: Vernon Lowerui

Product Manager: Dave Mason
Editorial Assitant: Rachel Guzmanji
Pedagogy: Debra Long
Cover Image: Jim Reed/Getty Images
Text and Cover Printer: City Printing, Inc.
Compositor: Media Mix, Inc.

For more information about our products, contact us at:
Dave.Mason@RicoPublications.com

For permission to use material from this text or product, submit a request online to:
Dave.Mason@RicoPublications.com

Printed in the United States
ISBN:

Contents

TO THE STUDENT

COMPREHENSIVE

The *MznLnx* Exam Prep series is designed to help you pass your exams. Editors at MznLnx review your textbooks and then prepare these practice exams to help you master the textbook material. Unlike study guides, workbooks, and practice tests provided by the texbook publisher and textbook authors, *MznLnx* gives you ***all*** of the material in each chapter in exam form, not just samples, so you can be sure to nail your exam.

MECHANICAL

The MznLnx Exam Prep series creates exams that will help you learn the subject matter as well as test you on your understanding. Each question is designed to help you master the concept. Just working through the exams, you gain an understanding of the subject--its a simple mechanical process that produces success.

INTEGRATED STUDY GUIDE AND REVIEW

MznLnx is not just a set of exams designed to test you, its also a comprehensive review of the subject content. Each exam question is also a review of the concept, making sure that you will get the answer correct without having to go to other sources of material. You learn as you go! Its the easiest way to pass an exam.

HUMOR

Studying can be tedious and dry. MznLnx's instructional design includes moderate humor within the exam questions on occassion, to break the tedium and revitalize the brain

1. _________ is defined by the American _________ Association as the activity, set of institutions, and processes for creating, communicating, delivering, and exchanging offerings that have value for customers, clients, partners, and society at large. The term developed from the original meaning which referred literally to going to market, as in shopping, or going to a market to sell goods or services.

_________ practice tends to be seen as a creative industry, which includes advertising, distribution and selling.

a. Customer acquisition management
b. Marketing
c. Product naming
d. Marketing myopia

2. Procter is a surname, and may also refer to:

- Bryan Waller Procter (pseud. Barry Cornwall), English poet
- Goodwin Procter, American law firm
- _________, consumer products multinational

.

a. Flyer
b. Black PRies
c. Convergent
d. Procter ' Gamble

3. A _________ is a systematic approach to selling a product or service. A growing body of published literature approaches the _________ from the point of view of an engineering discipline

Reasons for having a well thought-out _________ include seller and buyer risk management, standardized customer interaction in sales, and scalable revenue generation.

a. Sales process
b. Request for proposal
c. Lead generation
d. Sales management

4. _________ refer to a collection of facts usually collected as the result of experience, observation or experiment or a set of premises. This may consist of numbers, words particularly as measurements or observations of a set of variables. _________ are often viewed as a lowest level of abstraction from which information and knowledge are derived.

a. Mean
b. Pearson product-moment correlation coefficient
c. Sample size
d. Data

5. _________ is defined by the Oxford English Dictionary as 'the action or practice of selling among or between established clients, markets, traders, etc.' or 'that of selling an additional product or service to an existing customer'. In practice businesses define _________ in many different ways. Elements that might influence the definition might include: the size of the business, the industry sector it operates within and the financial motivations of those required to define the term.
a. Service provider
b. Cross-selling
c. Yield management
d. Freebie marketing

6. _________ is the set of reasons that determines one to engage in a particular behavior. The term is generally used for human _________ but, theoretically, it can be used to describe the causes for animal behavior as well
a. 180SearchAssistant
b. Power III
c. Role playing
d. Motivation

7. A _________ is a structured collection of records or data that is stored in a computer system. The structure is achieved by organizing the data according to a _________ model. The model in most common use today is the relational model.
a. Power III
b. 180SearchAssistant
c. 6-3-5 Brainwriting
d. Database

8. _________, originally the American Telephone ' Telegraph Company, is an American telecommunications company that provided voice, video, data, and Internet telecommunications and professional services to businesses, consumers, and government agencies. During its long history, AT'T was at times the world's largest telephone company, the world's largest cable television operator, and a regulated monopoly. Today, the company is a subsidiary of AT'T Inc.

a. ACNielsen
b. AMAX
c. ADTECH
d. AT'T Corporation

9. _________ is concerned with the provisions and use of accounting information to managers within organizations, to provide them with the basis to make informed business decisions that will allow them to be better equipped in their management and control functions.

In contrast to financial accountancy information, _________ information is:

- usually confidential and used by management, instead of publicly reported;
- forward-looking, instead of historical;
- pragmatically computed using extensive management information systems and internal controls, instead of complying with accounting standards.

This is because of the different emphasis: _________ information is used within an organization, typically for decision-making.

According to the Chartered Institute of Management Accountants (CIManagement accounting), _________ is 'the process of identification, measurement, accumulation, analysis, preparation, interpretation and communication of information used by management to plan, evaluate and control within an entity and to assure appropriate use of and accountability for its Resource (economics)resources. _________ also comprises the preparation of financial reports for non-management groups such as shareholders, creditors, regulatory agencies and tax authorities' (CIManagement accounting Official Terminology.)

a. Power III
b. Management accounting
c. 180SearchAssistant
d. 6-3-5 Brainwriting

10. _________ is the practice of individuals including commercial businesses, governments and institutions, facilitating the sale of their products or services to other companies or organizations that in turn resell them, use them as components in products or services they offer _________ is also called business-to-_________ for short. (Note that while marketing to government entities shares some of the same dynamics of organizational marketing, B2G Marketing is meaningfully different.)

a. Business marketing
b. Law of disruption
c. Mass marketing
d. Disruptive technology

11. _________ or _________ data refers to selected population characteristics as used in government, marketing or opinion research, or the _________ profiles used in such research. Note the distinction from the term 'demography' Commonly-used _________ include race, age, income, disabilities, mobility (in terms of travel time to work or number of vehicles available), educational attainment, home ownership, employment status, and even location.
a. AStore
b. African Americans
c. Albert Einstein
d. Demographic

12. _________ is the ability of an individual or group to seclude themselves or information about themselves and thereby reveal themselves selectively. The boundaries and content of what is considered private differ among cultures and individuals, but share basic common themes. _________ is sometimes related to anonymity, the wish to remain unnoticed or unidentified in the public realm.
a. Power III
b. 180SearchAssistant
c. 6-3-5 Brainwriting
d. Privacy

13. _________ is the physical search for minerals, fossils, precious metals or mineral specimens, and is also known as fossicking.

_________ is synonymous in some ways with mineral exploration which is an organised, large scale and at least semi-scientific effort undertaken by mineral resource companies to find commercially viable ore deposits. To actually be considered a prospector you must become registered as a professional prospector.

a. 180SearchAssistant
b. Power III
c. 6-3-5 Brainwriting
d. Prospecting

14. _________, or Value optimized pricing is a business strategy. It sets selling prices on the perceived value to the customer, rather than on the actual cost of the product, the market price, competitors prices, or the historical price.

The goal of _________ is to align price with value delivered.

a. Value-based pricing
b. Service-profit chain
c. Jobbing house
d. Money back guarantee

15. _________ in economics refers to metrics and measures of output from production processes, per unit of input. Labor _________, for example, is typically measured as a ratio of output per labor-hour, an input. _________ may be conceived of as a metrics of the technical or engineering efficiency of production.

a. Productivity
b. 180SearchAssistant
c. Value engineering
d. Power III

16. _________ is an advertisement in which a particular product specifically mentions a competitor by name for the express purpose of showing why the competitor is inferior to the product naming it.

This should not be confused with parody advertisements, where a fictional product is being advertised for the purpose of poking fun at the particular advertisement, nor should it be confused with the use of a coined brand name for the purpose of comparing the product without actually naming an actual competitor. ('Wikipedia tastes better and is less filling than the Encyclopedia Galactica.')

In the 1980s, during what has been referred to as the cola wars, soft-drink manufacturer Pepsi ran a series of advertisements where people, caught on hidden camera, in a blind taste test, chose Pepsi over rival Coca-Cola.

a. Cost per conversion
b. Comparative advertising
c. Heavy-up
d. GL-70

17. _________ refers to a range of skills, tools, and techniques utilized to accomplish specific tasks, projects and goals. This set encompass a wide scope of activities, and these include planning, setting goals, delegation, analysis of time spent, monitoring, organizing, scheduling, and prioritizing. Initially _________ referred to just business or work activities, but eventually the term broadened to include personal activities also.

a. Goal setting
b. Digital strategy
c. Time management
d. Business plan

18. _________ is the process of estimation in unknown situations. Prediction is a similar, but more general term. Both can refer to estimation of time series, cross-sectional or longitudinal data.
a. Power III
b. 6-3-5 Brainwriting
c. Forecasting
d. 180SearchAssistant

19. Human beings are also considered to be _________ because they have the ability to change raw materials into valuable _________. The term Human _________ can also be defined as the skills, energies, talents, abilities and knowledge that are used for the production of goods or the rendering of services. While taking into account human beings as _________, the following things have to be kept in mind:

- The size of the population
- The capabilities of the individuals in that population

Many _________ cannot be consumed in their original form. They have to be processed in order to change them into more usable commodities.

a. 6-3-5 Brainwriting
b. Power III
c. 180SearchAssistant
d. Resources

20. _________ is a recursive process where two or more people or organizations work together toward an intersection of common goals -- for example, an intellectual endeavor that is creative in nature--by sharing knowledge, learning and building consensus. _________ does not require leadership and can sometimes bring better results through decentralization and egalitarianism. In particular, teams that work collaboratively can obtain greater resources, recognition and reward when facing competition for finite resources._________ is also present in opposing goals exhibiting the notion of adversarial _________, though this notion is atypical of the annotation that people have given towards their understanding of _________.

a. Collaboration
b. Power III
c. 6-3-5 Brainwriting
d. 180SearchAssistant

1. _________ is defined by the American _________ Association as the activity, set of institutions, and processes for creating, communicating, delivering, and exchanging offerings that have value for customers, clients, partners, and society at large. The term developed from the original meaning which referred literally to going to market, as in shopping, or going to a market to sell goods or services.

_________ practice tends to be seen as a creative industry, which includes advertising, distribution and selling.

a. Customer acquisition management
b. Product naming
c. Marketing
d. Marketing myopia

2. _________ is a rivalry between individuals, groups, nations for territory, a niche, or allocation of resources. It arises whenever two or more parties strive for a goal which cannot be shared. _________ occurs naturally between living organisms which co-exist in the same environment.
a. Non-price competition
b. Price competition
c. Price fixing
d. Competition

3. Competitiveness is a comparative concept of the ability and performance of a firm, sub-sector or country to sell and supply goods and/or services in a given market. Although widely used in economics and business management, the usefulness of the concept, particularly in the context of national competitiveness, is vigorously disputed by economists, such as Paul Krugman .

The term may also be applied to markets, where it is used to refer to the extent to which the market structure may be regarded as perfectly _________.

a. Geographical pricing
b. Customs union
c. Free trade zone
d. Competitive

4. _________ is, in very basic words, a position a firm occupies against its competitors.

According to Michael Porter, the three methods for creating a sustainable _________ are through:

1. Cost leadership - Cost advantage occurs when a firm delivers the same services as its competitors but at a lower cost;

2.

a. Power III
b. 180SearchAssistant
c. 6-3-5 Brainwriting
d. Competitive advantage

5. Procter is a surname, and may also refer to:

- Bryan Waller Procter (pseud. Barry Cornwall), English poet
- Goodwin Procter, American law firm
- _________, consumer products multinational

.

a. Flyer
b. Convergent
c. Procter ' Gamble
d. Black PRies

6. A personal and cultural _________ is a relative ethic _________, an assumption upon which implementation can be extrapolated. A _________ system is a set of consistent _________s and measures that is soo not true. A principle _________ is a foundation upon which other _________s and measures of integrity are based.
a. Perceptual maps
b. Supreme Court of the United States
c. Package-on-Package
d. Value

7. In the field of marketing, a customer _________ consists of the sum total of benefits which a vendor promises that a customer will receive in return for the customer's associated payment (or other value-transfer.)

Put simply, the _________ is what the customer gets for his money.

Accordingly, a customer can evaluate a company's value-proposition on two broad dimensions with multiple subsets:

1. relative performance: what the customer gets from the vendor relative to a competitor's offering;
2. price: which consists of the payment the customer makes to acquire the product or service; plus the access cost

The vendor-company's marketing and sales efforts offer a customer _________; the vendor-company's delivery and customer-service processes then fulfill that value-proposition.

A value-proposition can assist in a firm's marketing strategy, and may guide a business to target a particular market segment.

a. DefCom Australia
b. Relationship management
c. Marketing performance measurement and management
d. Value proposition

8. The _________ is an independent agency of the United States government, established in 1914 by the _________ Act. Its principal mission is the promotion of 'consumer protection' and the elimination and prevention of what regulators perceive to be harmfully 'anti-competitive' business practices, such as coercive monopoly.

The _________ Act was one of President Wilson's major acts against trusts.

a. 6-3-5 Brainwriting
b. Federal Trade Commission
c. 180SearchAssistant
d. Power III

9. _________ is the ability of an individual or group to seclude themselves or information about themselves and thereby reveal themselves selectively. The boundaries and content of what is considered private differ among cultures and individuals, but share basic common themes. _________ is sometimes related to anonymity, the wish to remain unnoticed or unidentified in the public realm.

a. Privacy
b. Power III
c. 6-3-5 Brainwriting
d. 180SearchAssistant

10. _________ is difficult to define. For example, in 1952, Alfred Kroeber and Clyde Kluckhohn compiled a list of 164 definitions of '_________' in _________: A Critical Review of Concepts and Definitions. However, the word '_________' is most commonly used in three basic senses:

- excellence of taste in the fine arts and humanities
- an integrated pattern of human knowledge, belief, and behavior that depends upon the capacity for symbolic thought and social learning
- the set of shared attitudes, values, goals, and practices that characterizes an institution, organization or group.

When the concept first emerged in eighteenth- and nineteenth-century Europe, it connoted a process of cultivation or improvement, as in agriculture or horticulture. In the nineteenth century, it came to refer first to the betterment or refinement of the individual, especially through education, and then to the fulfillment of national aspirations or ideals.

a. AStore
b. Culture
c. African Americans
d. Albert Einstein

11. _________ is the corporate management term for the act of partially dismantling or otherwise reorganizing a company for the purpose of making it more profitable. Also known as corporate _________, debt _________ and financial _________.

_________ is often done as part of a bankruptcy or of a strategic takeover by another firm, such as a leveraged buyout by a private equity firm.

a. Restructuring
b. Market value
c. Power III
d. 180SearchAssistant

12. _________ is an advertisement in which a particular product specifically mentions a competitor by name for the express purpose of showing why the competitor is inferior to the product naming it.

This should not be confused with parody advertisements, where a fictional product is being advertised for the purpose of poking fun at the particular advertisement, nor should it be confused with the use of a coined brand name for the purpose of comparing the product without actually naming an actual competitor. ('Wikipedia tastes better and is less filling than the Encyclopedia Galactica.')

In the 1980s, during what has been referred to as the cola wars, soft-drink manufacturer Pepsi ran a series of advertisements where people, caught on hidden camera, in a blind taste test, chose Pepsi over rival Coca-Cola.

a. GL-70
b. Cost per conversion
c. Heavy-up
d. Comparative advertising

13. _________ is the collection, deployment and translation of information that allows a business to acquire, develop and retain their customers.

Firslty, the collected data must be audited to fully understand the quality and opportunity within the database. Once this is done, there are a number of different types of analysis that can be applied.

a. Societal marketing
b. Customer analytics
c. Fifth screen
d. Customer insight

14. Human beings are also considered to be _________ because they have the ability to change raw materials into valuable _________. The term Human _________ can also be defined as the skills, energies, talents, abilities and knowledge that are used for the production of goods or the rendering of services. While taking into account human beings as _________, the following things have to be kept in mind:

- The size of the population
- The capabilities of the individuals in that population

Many _________ cannot be consumed in their original form. They have to be processed in order to change them into more usable commodities.

a. 6-3-5 Brainwriting
b. Power III
c. Resources
d. 180SearchAssistant

15. Sales force management systems are information systems used in marketing and management that help automate some sales and sales force management functions. They are frequently combined with a marketing information system, in which case they are often called Customer Relationship Management (CRM) systems.

_________ Systems , typically a part of a company's customer relationship management system, is a system that automatically records all the stages in a sales process.

a. 6-3-5 Brainwriting
b. Sales force automation
c. Power III
d. 180SearchAssistant

16. _________ is the process whereby an organization establishes the parameters within which programs, investments, and acquisitions are reaching the desired results. Performance Reference Model of the Federal Enterprise Architecture, 2005.

This process of measuring performance often requires the use of statistical evidence to determine progress toward specific defined organizational objectives.

There are many types of measurements.

a. Voice of the customer
b. Performance measurement
c. Digital strategy
d. Crisis management

17. In marketing, _________ has come to mean the process by which marketers try to create an image or identity in the minds of their target market for its product, brand, or organization. It is the 'relative competitive comparison' their product occupies in a given market as perceived by the target market.

Re-_________ involves changing the identity of a product, relative to the identity of competing products, in the collective minds of the target market.

a. Positioning
b. GE matrix
c. Moratorium
d. Containerization

18. _________ is the realization of an application idea, model, design, specification, standard, algorithm an _________ is a realization of a technical specification or algorithm as a program, software component, or other computer system. Many _________s may exist for a given specification or standard.

a. AMAX
b. ACNielsen
c. Implementation
d. ADTECH

1. A personal and cultural _________ is a relative ethic _________, an assumption upon which implementation can be extrapolated. A _________ system is a set of consistent _________s and measures that is soo not true. A principle _________ is a foundation upon which other _________s and measures of integrity are based.

a. Package-on-Package
b. Value
c. Supreme Court of the United States
d. Perceptual maps

2. _________ is a branch of philosophy which seeks to address questions about morality, such as how a moral outcome can be achieved in a specific situation (applied _________), how moral values should be determined (normative _________), what moral values people actually abide by (descriptive _________), what the fundamental semantic, ontological, and epistemic nature of _________ or morality is (meta-_________), and how moral capacity or moral agency develops and what its nature is (moral psychology.)

Socrates was one of the first Greek philosophers to encourage both scholars and the common citizen to turn their attention from the outside world to the condition of man. In this view, Knowledge having a bearing on human life was placed highest, all other knowledge being secondary.

a. ACNielsen
b. ADTECH
c. Ethics
d. AMAX

3. In the social sciences, a _________ is a society where valuable goods and services are regularly given without any explicit agreement for immediate or future rewards (i.e. there is no visible quid pro quo). Ideally, simultaneous or recurring giving serves to circulate and redistribute valuables within the community. The organization of a _________ stands in contrast to a barter economy or a market economy.

a. Black market
b. Protectionism
c. Gift economy
d. Mixed economy

4. _________ can be regarded as an outcome of mental processes (cognitive process) leading to the selection of a course of action among several alternatives. Every _________ process produces a final choice. The output can be an action or an opinion of choice.

a. Power III
b. 180SearchAssistant
c. 6-3-5 Brainwriting
d. Decision making

5. Procter is a surname, and may also refer to:

- Bryan Waller Procter (pseud. Barry Cornwall), English poet
- Goodwin Procter, American law firm
- _________, consumer products multinational

a. Black PRies
b. Procter ' Gamble
c. Flyer
d. Convergent

6. An _________ is a person who creates or discovers a new method, form, device or other useful means. The word _________ comes form the latin verb invenire, invent-, to find. The system of patents was established to encourage _________s by granting limited-term, limited monopoly on inventions determined to be sufficiently novel, non-obvious, and useful.

a. ADTECH
b. AMAX
c. ACNielsen
d. Inventor

7. _________ is the ability of an individual or group to seclude themselves or information about themselves and thereby reveal themselves selectively. The boundaries and content of what is considered private differ among cultures and individuals, but share basic common themes. _________ is sometimes related to anonymity, the wish to remain unnoticed or unidentified in the public realm.

a. Privacy
b. 6-3-5 Brainwriting
c. 180SearchAssistant
d. Power III

8. _________ is the set of reasons that determines one to engage in a particular behavior. The term is generally used for human _________ but, theoretically, it can be used to describe the causes for animal behavior as well

a. Motivation
b. Role playing
c. 180SearchAssistant
d. Power III

9. _________ is a concept that denotes the precise probability of specific eventualities. Technically, the notion of _________ is independent from the notion of value and, as such, eventualities may have both beneficial and adverse consequences. However, in general usage the convention is to focus only on potential negative impact to some characteristic of value that may arise from a future event.

a. Power III
b. 6-3-5 Brainwriting
c. 180SearchAssistant
d. Risk

10. In psychology, philosophy, and the cognitive sciences, _________ is the process of attaining awareness or understanding of sensory information. It is a task far more complex than was imagined in the 1950s and 1960s, when it was predicted that building perceiving machines would take about a decade, a goal which is still very far from fruition. The word _________ comes from the Latin words _________, percepio, meaning 'receiving, collecting, action of taking possession, apprehension with the mind or senses.'

_________ is one of the oldest fields in psychology.

a. Perception
b. Groupthink
c. 180SearchAssistant
d. Power III

11. _________s is the social science that studies the production, distribution, and consumption of goods and services. The term _________s comes from the Ancient Greek οá¼°κονομÎ¯α from οá¼¶κος (oikos, 'house') + νÏŒμος (nomos, 'custom' or 'law'), hence 'rules of the house(hold)'. Current _________ models developed out of the broader field of political economy in the late 19th century, owing to a desire to use an empirical approach more akin to the physical sciences.

a. ACNielsen
b. Industrial organization
c. ADTECH
d. Economic

12. _________ in economics and business is the result of an exchange and from that trade we assign a numerical monetary value to a good, service or asset. If I trade 4 apples for an orange, the _________ of an orange is 4 - apples. Inversely, the _________ of an apple is 1/4 oranges.

a. Pricing
b. Discounts and allowances
c. Contribution margin-based pricing
d. Price

13. A _________ is a plan of action designed to achieve a particular goal.

_________ is different from tactics. In military terms, tactics is concerned with the conduct of an engagement while _________ is concerned with how different engagements are linked.

a. 6-3-5 Brainwriting
b. 180SearchAssistant
c. Power III
d. Strategy

14. _________ is defined by the American _________ Association as the activity, set of institutions, and processes for creating, communicating, delivering, and exchanging offerings that have value for customers, clients, partners, and society at large. The term developed from the original meaning which referred literally to going to market, as in shopping, or going to a market to sell goods or services.

_________ practice tends to be seen as a creative industry, which includes advertising, distribution and selling.

a. Marketing myopia
b. Marketing
c. Product naming
d. Customer acquisition management

15. _________ is a form of communication that typically attempts to persuade potential customers to purchase or to consume more of a particular brand of product or service. 'While now central to the contemporary global economy and the reproduction of global production networks, it is only quite recently that _________ has been more than a marginal influence on patterns of sales and production. The formation of modern _________ was intimately bound up with the emergence of new forms of monopoly capitalism around the end of the 19th and beginning of the 20th century as one element in corporate strategies to create, organize and where possible control markets, especially for mass produced consumer goods.
a. ACNielsen
b. AMAX
c. ADTECH
d. Advertising

16. _________ has been defined by the International Organization for Standardization (ISO) as 'ensuring that information is accessible only to those authorized to have access' and is one of the cornerstones of information security. _________ is one of the design goals for many cryptosystems, made possible in practice by the techniques of modern cryptography.

_________ also refers to an ethical principle associated with several professions (e.g., medicine, law, religion, professional psychology, and journalism.)

a. 180SearchAssistant
b. Power III
c. Confidentiality
d. 6-3-5 Brainwriting

17. _________ refer to a collection of facts usually collected as the result of experience, observation or experiment or a set of premises. This may consist of numbers, words particularly as measurements or observations of a set of variables. _________ are often viewed as a lowest level of abstraction from which information and knowledge are derived.
a. Mean
b. Pearson product-moment correlation coefficient
c. Sample size
d. Data

18. _________ is a form of applied ethics that examines ethical principles and moral or ethical problems that arise in a business environment. It applies to all aspects of business conduct and is relevant to the conduct of individuals and business organizations as a whole. Applied ethics is a field of ethics that deals with ethical questions in many fields such as medical, technical, legal and _________.
a. 6-3-5 Brainwriting
b. Power III
c. 180SearchAssistant
d. Business ethics

19. The _________ is an independent agency of the United States government, established in 1914 by the _________ Act. Its principal mission is the promotion of 'consumer protection' and the elimination and prevention of what regulators perceive to be harmfully 'anti-competitive' business practices, such as coercive monopoly.

The _________ Act was one of President Wilson's major acts against trusts.

a. 6-3-5 Brainwriting
b. Federal Trade Commission
c. Power III
d. 180SearchAssistant

1. In marketing, customer _________, lifetime customer value (LCV), or _________ (LTV) and a new concept of 'customer life cycle management' is the present value of the future cash flows attributed to the customer relationship. Use of customer _________ as a marketing metric tends to place greater emphasis on customer service and long-term customer satisfaction, rather than on maximizing short-term sales.

Customer _________ has intuitive appeal as a marketing concept, because in theory it represents exactly how much each customer is worth in monetary terms, and therefore exactly how much a marketing department should be willing to spend to acquire each customer.

a. Brand infiltration
b. Value chain
c. Sweepstakes
d. Lifetime value

2. A personal and cultural _________ is a relative ethic _________, an assumption upon which implementation can be extrapolated. A _________ system is a set of consistent _________s and measures that is soo not true. A principle _________ is a foundation upon which other _________s and measures of integrity are based.

a. Package-on-Package
b. Supreme Court of the United States
c. Perceptual maps
d. Value

3. _________ refer to a collection of facts usually collected as the result of experience, observation or experiment or a set of premises. This may consist of numbers, words particularly as measurements or observations of a set of variables. _________ are often viewed as a lowest level of abstraction from which information and knowledge are derived.

a. Pearson product-moment correlation coefficient
b. Sample size
c. Mean
d. Data

4. _________ consists of the processes a company uses to track and organize its contacts with its current and prospective customers. _________ software is used to support these processes; information about customers and customer interactions can be entered, stored and accessed by employees in different company departments. Typical _________ goals are to improve services provided to customers, and to use customer contact information for targeted marketing.

a. Demand generation
b. Commercialization
c. Product bundling
d. Customer relationship management

5. _________ is the activity that the selling organization undertakes to reduce customer account defections. The success of this activity is when the customer account places an additional order before a 12-month period has expired. Note that ideally these orders will need to contribute similar financial amounts to the previous 12 months.

a. Customer base
b. Customer retention
c. First-mover advantage
d. Customer centricity

6. Customer _________ consists of the processes a company uses to track and organize its contacts with its current and prospective customers. CRelationship management software is used to support these processes; information about customers and customer interactions can be entered, stored and accessed by employees in different company departments. Typical CRelationship management goals are to improve services provided to customers, and to use customer contact information for targeted marketing.

a. Marketing
b. Green marketing
c. Product bundling
d. Relationship management

7. _________, a business term, is a measure of how products and services supplied by a company meet or surpass customer expectation. It is seen as a key performance indicator within business and is part of the four perspectives of a Balanced Scorecard.

In a competitive marketplace where businesses compete for customers, _________ is seen as a key differentiator and increasingly has become a key element of business strategy.

a. Customer base
b. Customer satisfaction
c. Supplier diversity
d. Psychological pricing

8. _________, Gross profit margin or Gross Profit Rate can be defined as the amount of contribution to the business enterprise, after paying for direct-fixed and direct-variable unit costs, required to cover overheads (fixed commitments) and provide a buffer for unknown items. It expresses the relationship between gross profit and sales revenue.

It can be expressed in absolute terms:

Gross Profit = Revenue − Cost of Goods Sold

or as the ratio of gross profit to sales revenue, usually in the form of a percentage:

_________ Percentage = (Revenue-Cost of Goods Sold)/Revenue

Cost of goods sold includes variable costs and fixed costs directly linked to the product, such as material and labor.

a. 180SearchAssistant
b. Profit maximization
c. Power III
d. Gross margin

9. In economics, business, retail, and accounting, a _________ is the value of money that has been used up to produce something, and hence is not available for use anymore. In economics, a _________ is an alternative that is given up as a result of a decision. In business, the _________ may be one of acquisition, in which case the amount of money expended to acquire it is counted as _________.

a. Fixed costs
b. Transaction cost
c. Cost
d. Variable cost

10. In calculus, a function f defined on a subset of the real numbers with real values is called _________, if for all x and y such that x ≤ y one has f(x) ≤ f(y), so f preserves the order. In layman's terms, the sign of the slope is always positive (the curve tending upwards) or zero (i.e., non-decreasing, or asymptotic, or depicted as a horizontal, flat line) Likewise, a function is called monotonically decreasing (non-increasing) if, whenever x ≤ y, then f(x) ≥ f(y), so it reverses the order.

a. Power III
b. Monotonic
c. 180SearchAssistant
d. 6-3-5 Brainwriting

11. Procter is a surname, and may also refer to:

- Bryan Waller Procter (pseud. Barry Cornwall), English poet
- Goodwin Procter, American law firm
- _________, consumer products multinational

a. Flyer
b. Convergent
c. Black PRies
d. Procter ' Gamble

12. _________ is a broad label that refers to any individuals or households that use goods and services generated within the economy. The concept of a _________ is used in different contexts, so that the usage and significance of the term may vary.

A _________ is a person who uses any product or service.

a. Power III
b. 180SearchAssistant
c. 6-3-5 Brainwriting
d. Consumer

13. A _________ is a systematic approach to selling a product or service. A growing body of published literature approaches the _________ from the point of view of an engineering discipline

Reasons for having a well thought-out _________ include seller and buyer risk management, standardized customer interaction in sales, and scalable revenue generation.

a. Sales management
b. Request for proposal
c. Lead generation
d. Sales process

14. A _________ or logistics network is the system of organizations, people, technology, activities, information and resources involved in moving a product or service from supplier to customer. _________ activities transform natural resources, raw materials and components into a finished product that is delivered to the end customer. In sophisticated _________ systems, used products may re-enter the _________ at any point where residual value is recyclable.

a. Supply chain network
b. Demand chain management
c. Purchasing
d. Supply chain

15. _________ is one of the four elements of marketing mix. An organization or set of organizations (go-betweens) involved in the process of making a product or service available for use or consumption by a consumer or business user.

The other three parts of the marketing mix are product, pricing, and promotion.

a. Comparison-Shopping agent
b. Better Living Through Chemistry
c. Japan Advertising Photographers' Association
d. Distribution

16. _________ is a term that refers both to:

- a formal discipline used to help appraise, or assess, the case for a project or proposal, which itself is a process known as project appraisal; and
- an informal approach to making decisions of any kind.

Under both definitions the process involves, whether explicitly or implicitly, weighing the total expected costs against the total expected benefits of one or more actions in order to choose the best or most profitable option. The formal process is often referred to as either CBA (_________) or BCost-benefit analysis

A hallmark of CBA is that all benefits and all costs are expressed in money terms, and are adjusted for the time value of money, so that all flows of benefits and flows of project costs over time (which tend to occur at different points in time) are expressed on a common basis in terms of their 'present value.' Closely related, but slightly different, formal techniques include Cost-effectiveness analysis, Economic impact analysis, Fiscal impact analysis and Social Return on Investment(SROI) analysis. The latter builds upon the logic of _________, but differs in that it is explicitly designed to inform the practical decision-making of enterprise managers and investors focused on optimising their social and environmental impacts.

a. 180SearchAssistant
b. 6-3-5 Brainwriting
c. Cost-benefit analysis
d. Power III

17. _________ is an advertisement in which a particular product specifically mentions a competitor by name for the express purpose of showing why the competitor is inferior to the product naming it.

This should not be confused with parody advertisements, where a fictional product is being advertised for the purpose of poking fun at the particular advertisement, nor should it be confused with the use of a coined brand name for the purpose of comparing the product without actually naming an actual competitor. ('Wikipedia tastes better and is less filling than the Encyclopedia Galactica.')

In the 1980s, during what has been referred to as the cola wars, soft-drink manufacturer Pepsi ran a series of advertisements where people, caught on hidden camera, in a blind taste test, chose Pepsi over rival Coca-Cola.

a. GL-70
b. Comparative advertising
c. Heavy-up
d. Cost per conversion

18. _________ refers to the additional value of a commodity over the cost of commodities used to produce it from the previous stage of production. An example is the price of gasoline at the pump over the price of the oil in it. In national accounts used in macroeconomics, it refers to the contribution of the factors of production, i.e., land, labor, and capital goods, to raising the value of a product and corresponds to the incomes received by the owners of these factors. The factors of production provide 'services' which raise the unit price of a product (X) relative to the cost per unit of intermediate goods used up in the production of X. _________ is shared between the factors of production (capital, labor, also human capital), giving rise to issues of distribution.
a. Deregulation
b. Value added
c. Power III
d. Consumer spending

19. _________ is the process of estimation in unknown situations. Prediction is a similar, but more general term. Both can refer to estimation of time series, cross-sectional or longitudinal data.
a. Power III
b. 6-3-5 Brainwriting
c. Forecasting
d. 180SearchAssistant

1. Procter is a surname, and may also refer to:

- Bryan Waller Procter (pseud. Barry Cornwall), English poet
- Goodwin Procter, American law firm
- _________, consumer products multinational

.

a. Flyer
b. Procter ' Gamble
c. Black PRies
d. Convergent

2. Cognition is the scientific term for 'the process of thought.' Its usage varies in different ways in accord with different disciplines: For example, in psychology and _________ science it refers to an information processing view of an individual's psychological functions. Other interpretations of the meaning of cognition link it to the development of concepts; individual minds, groups, organizations, and even larger coalitions of entities, can be modelled as 'societies' (Society of Mind), which cooperate to form concepts.

The autonomous elements of each 'society' would have the opportunity to demonstrate emergent behavior in the face of some crisis or opportunity.

a. 6-3-5 Brainwriting
b. 180SearchAssistant
c. Power III
d. Cognitive

3. _________ is the set of reasons that determines one to engage in a particular behavior. The term is generally used for human _________ but, theoretically, it can be used to describe the causes for animal behavior as well

a. Motivation
b. Role playing
c. 180SearchAssistant
d. Power III

4. _________ is a form of social influence. It is the process of guiding people toward the adoption of an idea, attitude, or action by rational and symbolic (though not always logical) means. It is strategy of problem-solving relying on 'appeals' rather than coercion.

a. 180SearchAssistant
b. 6-3-5 Brainwriting
c. Power III
d. Persuasion

5. _________ is a term that has been used in various psychology theories, often in slightly different ways (e.g., Goldstein, Maslow, Rogers.) The term was originally introduced by the organismic theorist Kurt Goldstein for the motive to realise all of one's potentialities. In his view, it is the master motive--indeed, the only real motive a person has, all others being merely manifestations of it.
a. 180SearchAssistant
b. Self-actualization
c. Power III
d. 6-3-5 Brainwriting

6. Maslow's _________ is a theory in psychology, proposed by Abraham Maslow in his 1943 paper A Theory of Human Motivation, which he subsequently extended to include his observations of humans' innate curiosity.

Maslow studied what he called exemplary people such as Albert Einstein, Jane Addams, Eleanor Roosevelt, and Frederick Douglass rather than mentally ill or neurotic people, writing that 'the study of crippled, stunted, immature, and unhealthy specimens can yield only a cripple psychology and a cripple philosophy.' Maslow also studied the healthiest one percent of the college student population. In his book, The Farther Reaches of Human Nature, Maslow writes, 'By ordinary standards of this kind of laboratory research...

a. Hierarchy of needs
b. 6-3-5 Brainwriting
c. Power III
d. 180SearchAssistant

7. _________ is a measure of the strength of a brand, product, service relative to competitive offerings. There is often a geographic element to the competitive landscape. In defining _________, you must see to what extent a product, brand, or firm controls a product category in a given geographic area.
a. Productivity
b. Market system
c. Discretionary spending
d. Market dominance

8. _________ is the practice of individuals including commercial businesses, governments and institutions, facilitating the sale of their products or services to other companies or organizations that in turn resell them, use them as components in products or services they offer _________ is also called business-to-_________ for short. (Note that while marketing to government entities shares some of the same dynamics of organizational marketing, B2G Marketing is meaningfully different.)

a. Law of disruption
b. Mass marketing
c. Disruptive technology
d. Business marketing

9. _________ is the process of estimation in unknown situations. Prediction is a similar, but more general term. Both can refer to estimation of time series, cross-sectional or longitudinal data.

a. 6-3-5 Brainwriting
b. 180SearchAssistant
c. Forecasting
d. Power III

10. _________ is a concept that denotes the precise probability of specific eventualities. Technically, the notion of _________ is independent from the notion of value and, as such, eventualities may have both beneficial and adverse consequences. However, in general usage the convention is to focus only on potential negative impact to some characteristic of value that may arise from a future event.

a. 6-3-5 Brainwriting
b. Power III
c. Risk
d. 180SearchAssistant

11. In promotion and of advertising, a _________ or endorsement consists of a written or spoken statement, sometimes from a person figure, sometimes from a private citizen, extolling the virtue of some product. The term '_________' most commonly applies to the sales-pitches attributed to ordinary citizens, whereas 'endorsement' usually applies to pitches by celebrities. See also Testify, Testimony, for historical context and etymology.

a. Promotional products
b. Testimonial
c. Roll-in
d. Transpromotional

12. _________ is defined by the American _________ Association as the activity, set of institutions, and processes for creating, communicating, delivering, and exchanging offerings that have value for customers, clients, partners, and society at large. The term developed from the original meaning which referred literally to going to market, as in shopping, or going to a market to sell goods or services.

_________ practice tends to be seen as a creative industry, which includes advertising, distribution and selling.

a. Product naming
b. Marketing myopia
c. Customer acquisition management
d. Marketing

13. Sales force management systems are information systems used in marketing and management that help automate some sales and sales force management functions. They are frequently combined with a marketing information system, in which case they are often called Customer Relationship Management (CRM) systems.

_________ Systems , typically a part of a company's customer relationship management system, is a system that automatically records all the stages in a sales process.

a. Power III
b. 180SearchAssistant
c. Sales force automation
d. 6-3-5 Brainwriting

1. Procter is a surname, and may also refer to:

- Bryan Waller Procter (pseud. Barry Cornwall), English poet
- Goodwin Procter, American law firm
- _________, consumer products multinational

.

a. Convergent
b. Procter ' Gamble
c. Black PRies
d. Flyer

2. _________ is the physical search for minerals, fossils, precious metals or mineral specimens, and is also known as fossicking.

_________ is synonymous in some ways with mineral exploration which is an organised, large scale and at least semi-scientific effort undertaken by mineral resource companies to find commercially viable ore deposits. To actually be considered a prospector you must become registered as a professional prospector.

a. Power III
b. 180SearchAssistant
c. 6-3-5 Brainwriting
d. Prospecting

3. _________, originally the American Telephone ' Telegraph Company, is an American telecommunications company that provided voice, video, data, and Internet telecommunications and professional services to businesses, consumers, and government agencies. During its long history, AT'T was at times the world's largest telephone company, the world's largest cable television operator, and a regulated monopoly. Today, the company is a subsidiary of AT'T Inc.
a. ACNielsen
b. AT'T Corporation
c. AMAX
d. ADTECH

4. _________ is defined by the American _________ Association as the activity, set of institutions, and processes for creating, communicating, delivering, and exchanging offerings that have value for customers, clients, partners, and society at large. The term developed from the original meaning which referred literally to going to market, as in shopping, or going to a market to sell goods or services.

_________ practice tends to be seen as a creative industry, which includes advertising, distribution and selling.

a. Customer acquisition management
b. Product naming
c. Marketing myopia
d. Marketing

5. _________ in economics and business is the result of an exchange and from that trade we assign a numerical monetary value to a good, service or asset. If I trade 4 apples for an orange, the _________ of an orange is 4 - apples. Inversely, the _________ of an apple is 1/4 oranges.

a. Price
b. Discounts and allowances
c. Contribution margin-based pricing
d. Pricing

6. _________ is an advertisement in which a particular product specifically mentions a competitor by name for the express purpose of showing why the competitor is inferior to the product naming it.

This should not be confused with parody advertisements, where a fictional product is being advertised for the purpose of poking fun at the particular advertisement, nor should it be confused with the use of a coined brand name for the purpose of comparing the product without actually naming an actual competitor. ('Wikipedia tastes better and is less filling than the Encyclopedia Galactica.')

In the 1980s, during what has been referred to as the cola wars, soft-drink manufacturer Pepsi ran a series of advertisements where people, caught on hidden camera, in a blind taste test, chose Pepsi over rival Coca-Cola.

a. Heavy-up
b. Comparative advertising
c. GL-70
d. Cost per conversion

7. _________ is a rivalry between individuals, groups, nations for territory, a niche, or allocation of resources. It arises whenever two or more parties strive for a goal which cannot be shared. _________ occurs naturally between living organisms which co-exist in the same environment.

a. Price fixing
b. Price competition
c. Non-price competition
d. Competition

8. A _________ is a structured collection of records or data that is stored in a computer system. The structure is achieved by organizing the data according to a _________ model. The model in most common use today is the relational model.

a. Power III
b. Database
c. 6-3-5 Brainwriting
d. 180SearchAssistant

9. _________ is a list for goods and materials held available in stock by a business. It is also used for a list of the contents of a household and for a list for testamentary purposes of the possessions of someone who has died. In accounting _________ is considered an asset.

a. Inventory
b. Ending Inventory
c. ADTECH
d. ACNielsen

10. An _________ is a person who creates or discovers a new method, form, device or other useful means. The word _________ comes form the latin verb invenire, invent-, to find. The system of patents was established to encourage _________s by granting limited-term, limited monopoly on inventions determined to be sufficiently novel, non-obvious, and useful.

a. ACNielsen
b. Inventor
c. AMAX
d. ADTECH

11. Human beings are also considered to be _________ because they have the ability to change raw materials into valuable _________. The term Human _________ can also be defined as the skills, energies, talents, abilities and knowledge that are used for the production of goods or the rendering of services. While taking into account human beings as _________, the following things have to be kept in mind:

- The size of the population
- The capabilities of the individuals in that population

Many _________ cannot be consumed in their original form. They have to be processed in order to change them into more usable commodities.

a. 180SearchAssistant
b. 6-3-5 Brainwriting
c. Power III
d. Resources

12. _________ refer to a collection of facts usually collected as the result of experience, observation or experiment or a set of premises. This may consist of numbers, words particularly as measurements or observations of a set of variables. _________ are often viewed as a lowest level of abstraction from which information and knowledge are derived.
a. Sample size
b. Mean
c. Pearson product-moment correlation coefficient
d. Data

13. _________ , according to Cornish, 'the process of acquiring and analyzing information in order to understand the market (both existing and potential customers); to determine the current and future needs and preferences, attitudes and behavior of the market; and to assess changes in the business environment that may affect the size and nature of the market in the future.' ('Product', 1997, p147.)

This figure shows how the interaction between variables from producers, communication channels, and consumers vary the effectiveness of _________ which affects the performance of the sales of a new product. The product is central in a circle because it helps to direct what information is gathered and how.

a. Brand parity
b. Market intelligence
c. Line extension
d. Co-branding

14. An _________ is a special-purpose computer system designed to perform one or a few dedicated functions, often with real-time computing constraints. It is usually embedded as part of a complete device including hardware and mechanical parts. In contrast, a general-purpose computer, such as a personal computer, can do many different tasks depending on programming.
a. ADTECH
b. ACNielsen
c. AMAX
d. Embedded system

15. In economics and sociology, an _________ is any factor (financial or non-financial) that enables or motivates a particular course of action, or counts as a reason for preferring one choice to the alternatives. It is an expectation that encourages people to behave in a certain way. Since human beings are purposeful creatures, the study of _________ structures is central to the study of all economic activity (both in terms of individual decision-making and in terms of co-operation and competition within a larger institutional structure.)

a. AMAX
b. ADTECH
c. ACNielsen
d. Incentive

16. A trade fair (trade show or expo) is an exhibition organized so that companies in a specific industry can showcase and demonstrate their latest products, service, study activities of rivals and examine recent trends and opportunities. Some trade fairs are open to the public, while others can only be attended by company representatives (members of the trade) and members of the press, therefore _________ are classified as either 'Public' or 'Trade Only'. They are held on a continuing basis in virtually all markets and normally attract companies from around the globe.

a. Power III
b. 6-3-5 Brainwriting
c. 180SearchAssistant
d. Trade shows

17. _________ is anything that is generally accepted as payment for goods and services and repayment of debts. The main uses of _________ are as a medium of exchange, a unit of account, and a store of value. Some authors explicitly require _________ to be a standard of deferred payment.

a. Money
b. Microeconomics
c. Law of supply
d. Leading indicator

1. _________ is defined by the American _________ Association as the activity, set of institutions, and processes for creating, communicating, delivering, and exchanging offerings that have value for customers, clients, partners, and society at large. The term developed from the original meaning which referred literally to going to market, as in shopping, or going to a market to sell goods or services.

_________ practice tends to be seen as a creative industry, which includes advertising, distribution and selling.

a. Product naming
b. Marketing myopia
c. Customer acquisition management
d. Marketing

2. Procter is a surname, and may also refer to:

- Bryan Waller Procter (pseud. Barry Cornwall), English poet
- Goodwin Procter, American law firm
- _________, consumer products multinational

.

a. Flyer
b. Convergent
c. Black PRies
d. Procter ' Gamble

3. _________ is the process of estimation in unknown situations. Prediction is a similar, but more general term. Both can refer to estimation of time series, cross-sectional or longitudinal data.
a. 180SearchAssistant
b. Forecasting
c. Power III
d. 6-3-5 Brainwriting

4. Human beings are also considered to be _________ because they have the ability to change raw materials into valuable _________. The term Human _________ can also be defined as the skills, energies, talents, abilities and knowledge that are used for the production of goods or the rendering of services. While taking into account human beings as _________, the following things have to be kept in mind:

- The size of the population
- The capabilities of the individuals in that population

Many _________ cannot be consumed in their original form. They have to be processed in order to change them into more usable commodities.

a. Power III
b. 180SearchAssistant
c. 6-3-5 Brainwriting
d. Resources

5. _________ refer to a collection of facts usually collected as the result of experience, observation or experiment or a set of premises. This may consist of numbers, words particularly as measurements or observations of a set of variables. _________ are often viewed as a lowest level of abstraction from which information and knowledge are derived.

a. Mean
b. Sample size
c. Pearson product-moment correlation coefficient
d. Data

1. Procter is a surname, and may also refer to:

- Bryan Waller Procter (pseud. Barry Cornwall), English poet
- Goodwin Procter, American law firm
- _________, consumer products multinational

.

a. Procter ' Gamble
b. Black PRies
c. Convergent
d. Flyer

2. _________ is a fee paid on borrowed assets. It is the price paid for the use of borrowed money , or, money earned by deposited funds . Assets that are sometimes lent with _________ include money, shares, consumer goods through hire purchase, major assets such as aircraft, and even entire factories in finance lease arrangements.

a. ACNielsen
b. Interest
c. AMAX
d. ADTECH

3. The _________ is an independent agency of the United States government, established in 1914 by the _________ Act. Its principal mission is the promotion of 'consumer protection' and the elimination and prevention of what regulators perceive to be harmfully 'anti-competitive' business practices, such as coercive monopoly.

The _________ Act was one of President Wilson's major acts against trusts.

a. 6-3-5 Brainwriting
b. Federal Trade Commission
c. Power III
d. 180SearchAssistant

4. _________ describes the situation when output from (or information about the result of) an event or phenomenon in the past will influence the same event/phenomenon in the present or future. When an event is part of a chain of cause-and-effect that forms a circuit or loop, then the event is said to 'feed back' into itself.

_________ is also a synonym for:

- _________ Signal; the information about the initial event that is the basis for subsequent modification of the event.
- _________ Loop; the causal path that leads from the initial generation of the _________ signal to the subsequent modification of the event.

_________ is a mechanism, process or signal that is looped back to control a system within itself. Such a loop is called a _________ loop.

a. 180SearchAssistant
b. 6-3-5 Brainwriting
c. Feedback
d. Power III

5. _________ is the ability of an individual or group to seclude themselves or information about themselves and thereby reveal themselves selectively. The boundaries and content of what is considered private differ among cultures and individuals, but share basic common themes. _________ is sometimes related to anonymity, the wish to remain unnoticed or unidentified in the public realm.
a. 6-3-5 Brainwriting
b. Privacy
c. Power III
d. 180SearchAssistant

6. _________ is an advertisement in which a particular product specifically mentions a competitor by name for the express purpose of showing why the competitor is inferior to the product naming it.

This should not be confused with parody advertisements, where a fictional product is being advertised for the purpose of poking fun at the particular advertisement, nor should it be confused with the use of a coined brand name for the purpose of comparing the product without actually naming an actual competitor. ('Wikipedia tastes better and is less filling than the Encyclopedia Galactica.')

In the 1980s, during what has been referred to as the cola wars, soft-drink manufacturer Pepsi ran a series of advertisements where people, caught on hidden camera, in a blind taste test, chose Pepsi over rival Coca-Cola.

a. Comparative advertising
b. GL-70
c. Heavy-up
d. Cost per conversion

1. _________ is defined by the American _________ Association as the activity, set of institutions, and processes for creating, communicating, delivering, and exchanging offerings that have value for customers, clients, partners, and society at large. The term developed from the original meaning which referred literally to going to market, as in shopping, or going to a market to sell goods or services.

_________ practice tends to be seen as a creative industry, which includes advertising, distribution and selling.

a. Marketing myopia
b. Product naming
c. Customer acquisition management
d. Marketing

2. Procter is a surname, and may also refer to:

- Bryan Waller Procter (pseud. Barry Cornwall), English poet
- Goodwin Procter, American law firm
- _________, consumer products multinational

.

a. Black PRies
b. Procter ' Gamble
c. Convergent
d. Flyer

3. _________ refer to a collection of facts usually collected as the result of experience, observation or experiment or a set of premises. This may consist of numbers, words particularly as measurements or observations of a set of variables. _________ are often viewed as a lowest level of abstraction from which information and knowledge are derived.

a. Pearson product-moment correlation coefficient
b. Mean
c. Data
d. Sample size

4. An _________ is a person who creates or discovers a new method, form, device or other useful means. The word _________ comes form the latin verb invenire, invent-, to find. The system of patents was established to encourage _________s by granting limited-term, limited monopoly on inventions determined to be sufficiently novel, non-obvious, and useful.

a. ACNielsen
b. AMAX
c. ADTECH
d. Inventor

5. _________ is a list for goods and materials held available in stock by a business. It is also used for a list of the contents of a household and for a list for testamentary purposes of the possessions of someone who has died. In accounting _________ is considered an asset.

a. Ending Inventory
b. ADTECH
c. Inventory
d. ACNielsen

6. A _________ or pamphlet is a leaflet advertisement. _________s may advertise locations, events, hotels, products, services, etc. They are usually succinct in language and eye-catching in design.

a. Brochure
b. Marketspace
c. Sweepstakes
d. Customer relationship management

7. _________ is a form of social influence. It is the process of guiding people toward the adoption of an idea, attitude, or action by rational and symbolic (though not always logical) means. It is strategy of problem-solving relying on 'appeals' rather than coercion.

a. Power III
b. 180SearchAssistant
c. 6-3-5 Brainwriting
d. Persuasion

8. In promotion and of advertising, a _________ or endorsement consists of a written or spoken statement, sometimes from a person figure, sometimes from a private citizen, extolling the virtue of some product. The term '_________' most commonly applies to the sales-pitches attributed to ordinary citizens, whereas 'endorsement' usually applies to pitches by celebrities. See also Testify, Testimony, for historical context and etymology.

a. Testimonial
b. Roll-in
c. Transpromotional
d. Promotional products

9. Human beings are also considered to be _________ because they have the ability to change raw materials into valuable _________. The term Human _________ can also be defined as the skills, energies, talents, abilities and knowledge that are used for the production of goods or the rendering of services. While taking into account human beings as _________, the following things have to be kept in mind:

- The size of the population
- The capabilities of the individuals in that population

Many _________ cannot be consumed in their original form. They have to be processed in order to change them into more usable commodities.

a. Power III
b. 180SearchAssistant
c. 6-3-5 Brainwriting
d. Resources

10. A _________ is a systematic approach to selling a product or service. A growing body of published literature approaches the _________ from the point of view of an engineering discipline

Reasons for having a well thought-out _________ include seller and buyer risk management, standardized customer interaction in sales, and scalable revenue generation.

a. Lead generation
b. Request for proposal
c. Sales management
d. Sales process

1. _________ is defined by the American _________ Association as the activity, set of institutions, and processes for creating, communicating, delivering, and exchanging offerings that have value for customers, clients, partners, and society at large. The term developed from the original meaning which referred literally to going to market, as in shopping, or going to a market to sell goods or services.

_________ practice tends to be seen as a creative industry, which includes advertising, distribution and selling.

a. Marketing
b. Product naming
c. Marketing myopia
d. Customer acquisition management

2. _________ is the set of reasons that determines one to engage in a particular behavior. The term is generally used for human _________ but, theoretically, it can be used to describe the causes for animal behavior as well

a. Power III
b. 180SearchAssistant
c. Motivation
d. Role playing

3. _________s is the social science that studies the production, distribution, and consumption of goods and services. The term _________s comes from the Ancient Greek οá¼°κονομΙ¯α from οá¼¶κος (oikos, 'house') + νÏŒμος (nomos, 'custom' or 'law'), hence 'rules of the house(hold)'. Current _________ models developed out of the broader field of political economy in the late 19th century, owing to a desire to use an empirical approach more akin to the physical sciences.

a. ADTECH
b. Industrial organization
c. Economic
d. ACNielsen

4. The _________ of a good or service has puzzled economists since the beginning of the discipline. First, economists tried to estimate the value of a good to an individual alone, and extend that definition to goods which can be exchanged. From this analysis came the concepts value in use and value in exchange.

a. ADTECH
b. ACNielsen
c. AMAX
d. Economic value

5. A personal and cultural _________ is a relative ethic _________, an assumption upon which implementation can be extrapolated. A _________ system is a set of consistent _________s and measures that is soo not true. A principle _________ is a foundation upon which other _________s and measures of integrity are based.

a. Package-on-Package
b. Perceptual maps
c. Value
d. Supreme Court of the United States

6. Procter is a surname, and may also refer to:

- Bryan Waller Procter (pseud. Barry Cornwall), English poet
- Goodwin Procter, American law firm
- _________, consumer products multinational

.

a. Flyer
b. Black PRies
c. Convergent
d. Procter ' Gamble

7. Competitiveness is a comparative concept of the ability and performance of a firm, sub-sector or country to sell and supply goods and/or services in a given market. Although widely used in economics and business management, the usefulness of the concept, particularly in the context of national competitiveness, is vigorously disputed by economists, such as Paul Krugman .

The term may also be applied to markets, where it is used to refer to the extent to which the market structure may be regarded as perfectly _________.

a. Geographical pricing
b. Free trade zone
c. Competitive
d. Customs union

8. _________ is, in very basic words, a position a firm occupies against its competitors.

According to Michael Porter, the three methods for creating a sustainable _________ are through:

1. Cost leadership - Cost advantage occurs when a firm delivers the same services as its competitors but at a lower cost;

2.

a. Power III
b. Competitive advantage
c. 6-3-5 Brainwriting
d. 180SearchAssistant

9. In statistics, an _________ is a term in a statistical model added when the effect of two or more variables is not simply additive. Such a term reflects that the effect of one variable depends on the values of one or more other variables.

Thus, for a response Y and two variables x_1 and x_2 an additive model would be:

$$Y = ax_1 + bx_2 + \text{error}$$

In contrast to this,

$$Y = ax_1 + bx_2 + c(x_1 \times x_2) + \text{error},$$

is an example of a model with an _________ between variables x_1 and x_2 ('error' refers to the random variable whose value by which y differs from the expected value of y.)

a. AMAX
b. ACNielsen
c. Interaction
d. ADTECH

10. A _________ is a systematic approach to selling a product or service. A growing body of published literature approaches the _________ from the point of view of an engineering discipline

Reasons for having a well thought-out _________ include seller and buyer risk management, standardized customer interaction in sales, and scalable revenue generation.

a. Sales process
b. Lead generation
c. Sales management
d. Request for proposal

11. An _________ is quite usually a standard guarantee from the seller of a product that specifies the extent to which the quality or performance of the product is assured and states the conditions under which the product can be returned, replaced, or repaired. It is often given in the form of a specific, written 'Warranty' document. However, a warranty may also arise by operation of law based upon the seller's description of the goods, and perhaps their source and quality, and any material deviation from that specification would violate the guarantee.

a. Energy Star
b. Imperial Group v. Philip Morris
c. Office for Harmonization in the Internal Market
d. Express warranty

12. _________ is the imitation of some real thing, state of affairs, or process. The act of simulating something generally entails representing certain key characteristics or behaviors of a selected physical or abstract system.

_________ is used in many contexts, including the modeling of natural systems or human systems in order to gain insight into their functioning.

a. 6-3-5 Brainwriting
b. Power III
c. 180SearchAssistant
d. Simulation

1. _________ is defined by the American _________ Association as the activity, set of institutions, and processes for creating, communicating, delivering, and exchanging offerings that have value for customers, clients, partners, and society at large. The term developed from the original meaning which referred literally to going to market, as in shopping, or going to a market to sell goods or services.

_________ practice tends to be seen as a creative industry, which includes advertising, distribution and selling.

a. Product naming
b. Marketing
c. Customer acquisition management
d. Marketing myopia

2. In economic models, the _________ time frame assumes no fixed factors of production. Firms can enter or leave the marketplace, and the cost (and availability) of land, labor, raw materials, and capital goods can be assumed to vary. In contrast, in the short-run time frame, certain factors are assumed to be fixed, because there is not sufficient time for them to change.
a. 6-3-5 Brainwriting
b. 180SearchAssistant
c. Power III
d. Long-run

3. Procter is a surname, and may also refer to:

- Bryan Waller Procter (pseud. Barry Cornwall), English poet
- Goodwin Procter, American law firm
- _________, consumer products multinational

.

a. Flyer
b. Black PRies
c. Convergent
d. Procter ' Gamble

4 _________ can be regarded as an outcome of mental processes (cognitive process) leading to the selection of a course of action among several alternatives. Every _________ process produces a final choice. The output can be an action or an opinion of choice.

a. Decision making
b. 6-3-5 Brainwriting
c. Power III
d. 180SearchAssistant

5. _________ is a way of expressing knowledge or belief that an event will occur or has occurred. In mathematics the concept has been given an exact meaning in _________ theory, that is used extensively in such areas of study as mathematics, statistics, finance, gambling, science, and philosophy to draw conclusions about the likelihood of potential events and the underlying mechanics of complex systems.
a. Data
b. Heteroskedastic
c. Linear regression
d. Probability

6. _________ in economics and business is the result of an exchange and from that trade we assign a numerical monetary value to a good, service or asset. If I trade 4 apples for an orange, the _________ of an orange is 4 - apples. Inversely, the _________ of an apple is 1/4 oranges.
a. Pricing
b. Discounts and allowances
c. Price
d. Contribution margin-based pricing

7. A _________ is a systematic approach to selling a product or service. A growing body of published literature approaches the _________ from the point of view of an engineering discipline

Reasons for having a well thought-out _________ include seller and buyer risk management, standardized customer interaction in sales, and scalable revenue generation.

a. Lead generation
b. Sales process
c. Sales management
d. Request for proposal

8. _________ refer to a collection of facts usually collected as the result of experience, observation or experiment or a set of premises. This may consist of numbers, words particularly as measurements or observations of a set of variables. _________ are often viewed as a lowest level of abstraction from which information and knowledge are derived.

a. Data
b. Pearson product-moment correlation coefficient
c. Sample size
d. Mean

9. A _________ is a device that determines if a piece of currency is counterfeit. These devices are used in vending machines that accept payment and dispense a product to a customer. They are also used in change machines and in slot machines.
a. Power III
b. 180SearchAssistant
c. 6-3-5 Brainwriting
d. Currency detector

10. _________ is an advertisement in which a particular product specifically mentions a competitor by name for the express purpose of showing why the competitor is inferior to the product naming it.

This should not be confused with parody advertisements, where a fictional product is being advertised for the purpose of poking fun at the particular advertisement, nor should it be confused with the use of a coined brand name for the purpose of comparing the product without actually naming an actual competitor. ('Wikipedia tastes better and is less filling than the Encyclopedia Galactica.')

In the 1980s, during what has been referred to as the cola wars, soft-drink manufacturer Pepsi ran a series of advertisements where people, caught on hidden camera, in a blind taste test, chose Pepsi over rival Coca-Cola.

a. GL-70
b. Cost per conversion
c. Heavy-up
d. Comparative advertising

11. A _________ is a research instrument consisting of a series of questions and other prompts for the purpose of gathering information from respondents. Although they are often designed for statistical analysis of the responses, this is not always the case. The _________ was invented by Sir Francis Galton.
a. Mystery shoppers
b. Mystery shopping
c. Questionnaire
d. Market research

12.

The net present value (NPV) of all of a company's customers in terms of customer loyalty and indirectly, the revenue that the company can obtain from them.

In deciding the value of a company, it is important to know of how much value its customer base is in terms of future revenues. The greater the _________ , the more future revenue in the lifetime of its clients; this means that a company with a higher _________ can get more money from its customers on average than another company that is identical in all other characteristics.

a. Total cost
b. Marginal revenue
c. Product proliferation
d. Customer equity

13. A _________ is a type of business entity in which partners (owners) share with each other the profits or losses of the business undertaking in which all have invested. _________s are often favored over corporations for taxation purposes, as the _________ structure does not generally incur a tax on profits before it is distributed to the partners (i.e. there is no dividend tax levied.) However, depending on the _________ structure and the jurisdiction in which it operates, owners of a _________ may be exposed to greater personal liability than they would as shareholders of a corporation.

a. Brand piracy
b. Competition law
c. Partnership
d. Fair Debt Collection Practices Act

14. A supply chain is the system of organizations, people, technology, activities, information and resources involved in moving a product or service from _________ to customer. Supply chain activities transform natural resources, raw materials and components into a finished product that is delivered to the end customer. In sophisticated supply chain systems, used products may re-enter the supply chain at any point where residual value is recyclable.

a. Bringin' Home the Oil
b. Rebate
c. Supplier
d. Product line extension

1. _________ refer to a collection of facts usually collected as the result of experience, observation or experiment or a set of premises. This may consist of numbers, words particularly as measurements or observations of a set of variables. _________ are often viewed as a lowest level of abstraction from which information and knowledge are derived.

a. Pearson product-moment correlation coefficient
b. Mean
c. Sample size
d. Data

2. _________ is concerned with the provisions and use of accounting information to managers within organizations, to provide them with the basis to make informed business decisions that will allow them to be better equipped in their management and control functions.

In contrast to financial accountancy information, _________ information is:

- usually confidential and used by management, instead of publicly reported;
- forward-looking, instead of historical;
- pragmatically computed using extensive management information systems and internal controls, instead of complying with accounting standards.

This is because of the different emphasis: _________ information is used within an organization, typically for decision-making.

According to the Chartered Institute of Management Accountants (CIManagement accounting), _________ is 'the process of identification, measurement, accumulation, analysis, preparation, interpretation and communication of information used by management to plan, evaluate and control within an entity and to assure appropriate use of and accountability for its Resource (economics)resources. _________ also comprises the preparation of financial reports for non-management groups such as shareholders, creditors, regulatory agencies and tax authorities' (CIManagement accounting Official Terminology.)

a. 180SearchAssistant
b. Power III
c. 6-3-5 Brainwriting
d. Management accounting

3. Procter is a surname, and may also refer to:

- Bryan Waller Procter (pseud. Barry Cornwall), English poet
- Goodwin Procter, American law firm
- _________, consumer products multinational

.

a. Procter ' Gamble
b. Flyer
c. Convergent
d. Black PRies

4. A _________ is a list of the general tasks and responsibilities of a position. Typically, it also includes to whom the position reports, specifications such as the qualifications needed by the person in the job, salary range for the position, etc. A _________ is usually developed by conducting a job analysis, which includes examining the tasks and sequences of tasks necessary to perform the job.
a. 6-3-5 Brainwriting
b. Power III
c. Job description
d. 180SearchAssistant

5. _________ refers to a business or organization attempting to acquire goods or services to accomplish the goals of the enterprise. Though there are several organizations that attempt to set standards in the _________ process, processes can vary greatly between organizations. Typically the word '_________' is not used interchangeably with the word 'procurement', since procurement typically includes Expediting, Supplier Quality, and Traffic and Logistics (T'L) in addition to _________.
a. Supply chain
b. Supply network
c. Drop shipping
d. Purchasing

6. _________ in organizations and public policy is both the organizational process of creating and maintaining a plan; and the psychological process of thinking about the activities required to create a desired goal on some scale. As such, it is a fundamental property of intelligent behavior. This thought process is essential to the creation and refinement of a plan, or integration of it with other plans, that is, it combines forecasting of developments with the preparation of scenarios of how to react to them.
a. 6-3-5 Brainwriting
b. 180SearchAssistant
c. Planning
d. Power III

7. _________ is the realization of an application idea, model, design, specification, standard, algorithm an _________ is a realization of a technical specification or algorithm as a program, software component, or other computer system. Many _________s may exist for a given specification or standard.

a. AMAX
b. ADTECH
c. ACNielsen
d. Implementation

8. _________ is a term commonly used to describe commerce transactions between businesses like the one between a manufacturer and a wholesaler or a wholesaler and a retailer i.e both the buyer and the seller are business entity.This is unlike business-to-consumers (B2C) which involve a business entity and end consumer, or business-to-government (B2G) which involve a business entity and government.

The volume of B2B transactions is much higher than the volume of B2C transactions. The primary reason for this is that in a typical supply chain there will be many B2B transactions involving subcomponent or raw materials, and only one B2C transaction, specifically sale of the finished product to the end customer.

a. Social marketing
b. Customer relationship management
c. Business-to-business
d. Disruptive technology

9. A personal and cultural _________ is a relative ethic _________, an assumption upon which implementation can be extrapolated. A _________ system is a set of consistent _________s and measures that is soo not true. A principle _________ is a foundation upon which other _________s and measures of integrity are based.

a. Value
b. Package-on-Package
c. Supreme Court of the United States
d. Perceptual maps

1. _________ refer to a collection of facts usually collected as the result of experience, observation or experiment or a set of premises. This may consist of numbers, words particularly as measurements or observations of a set of variables. _________ are often viewed as a lowest level of abstraction from which information and knowledge are derived.

a. Pearson product-moment correlation coefficient
b. Sample size
c. Mean
d. Data

2. _________ refers to a range of skills, tools, and techniques utilized to accomplish specific tasks, projects and goals. This set encompass a wide scope of activities, and these include planning, setting goals, delegation, analysis of time spent, monitoring, organizing, scheduling, and prioritizing. Initially _________ referred to just business or work activities, but eventually the term broadened to include personal activities also.

a. Business plan
b. Goal setting
c. Time management
d. Digital strategy

3. _________ is the ability of an individual or group to seclude themselves or information about themselves and thereby reveal themselves selectively. The boundaries and content of what is considered private differ among cultures and individuals, but share basic common themes. _________ is sometimes related to anonymity, the wish to remain unnoticed or unidentified in the public realm.

a. 180SearchAssistant
b. Power III
c. 6-3-5 Brainwriting
d. Privacy

4. A _________ is a systematic approach to selling a product or service. A growing body of published literature approaches the _________ from the point of view of an engineering discipline

Reasons for having a well thought-out _________ include seller and buyer risk management, standardized customer interaction in sales, and scalable revenue generation.

a. Request for proposal
b. Lead generation
c. Sales management
d. Sales process

5. _________ is the term used to describe a situation where different entities cooperate advantageously for a final outcome. Simply defined, it means that the whole is greater than the sum of its parts. The essence of _________ is to value differences.

a. Synergy
b. Power III
c. 6-3-5 Brainwriting
d. 180SearchAssistant

6. Procter is a surname, and may also refer to:

- Bryan Waller Procter (pseud. Barry Cornwall), English poet
- Goodwin Procter, American law firm
- _________, consumer products multinational

.

a. Flyer
b. Convergent
c. Procter ' Gamble
d. Black PRies

7. A personal and cultural _________ is a relative ethic _________, an assumption upon which implementation can be extrapolated. A _________ system is a set of consistent _________s and measures that is soo not true. A principle _________ is a foundation upon which other _________s and measures of integrity are based.

a. Supreme Court of the United States
b. Package-on-Package
c. Perceptual maps
d. Value

8. _________ in economics refers to metrics and measures of output from production processes, per unit of input. Labor _________, for example, is typically measured as a ratio of output per labor-hour, an input. _________ may be conceived of as a metrics of the technical or engineering efficiency of production.

a. Power III
b. 180SearchAssistant
c. Value engineering
d. Productivity

9. _________ is a term used to describe the phenomenon of a marketplace being full or even overcrowded with products. It also refers to the extreme amount of advertising the average American sees in their daily lives. _________ is a major problem for marketers and advertisers.

a. Procter ' Gamble
b. Consumption Map
c. Push
d. Clutter

10. _________ is one of the four elements of marketing mix. An organization or set of organizations (go-betweens) involved in the process of making a product or service available for use or consumption by a consumer or business user.

The other three parts of the marketing mix are product, pricing, and promotion.

a. Japan Advertising Photographers' Association
b. Distribution
c. Comparison-Shopping agent
d. Better Living Through Chemistry

11. _________ is defined by the American _________ Association as the activity, set of institutions, and processes for creating, communicating, delivering, and exchanging offerings that have value for customers, clients, partners, and society at large. The term developed from the original meaning which referred literally to going to market, as in shopping, or going to a market to sell goods or services.

_________ practice tends to be seen as a creative industry, which includes advertising, distribution and selling.

a. Customer acquisition management
b. Marketing myopia
c. Product naming
d. Marketing

12. _________ consists of the processes a company uses to track and organize its contacts with its current and prospective customers. _________ software is used to support these processes; information about customers and customer interactions can be entered, stored and accessed by employees in different company departments. Typical _________ goals are to improve services provided to customers, and to use customer contact information for targeted marketing.

a. Commercialization
b. Demand generation
c. Product bundling
d. Customer relationship management

13. Customer _________ consists of the processes a company uses to track and organize its contacts with its current and prospective customers. CRelationship management software is used to support these processes; information about customers and customer interactions can be entered, stored and accessed by employees in different company departments. Typical CRelationship management goals are to improve services provided to customers, and to use customer contact information for targeted marketing.
a. Product bundling
b. Green marketing
c. Marketing
d. Relationship management

14. Sales force management systems are information systems used in marketing and management that help automate some sales and sales force management functions. They are frequently combined with a marketing information system, in which case they are often called Customer Relationship Management (CRM) systems.

_________ Systems , typically a part of a company's customer relationship management system, is a system that automatically records all the stages in a sales process.

a. 6-3-5 Brainwriting
b. Sales force automation
c. Power III
d. 180SearchAssistant

15. Human beings are also considered to be _________ because they have the ability to change raw materials into valuable _________. The term Human _________ can also be defined as the skills, energies, talents, abilities and knowledge that are used for the production of goods or the rendering of services. While taking into account human beings as _________, the following things have to be kept in mind:

- The size of the population
- The capabilities of the individuals in that population

Many _________ cannot be consumed in their original form. They have to be processed in order to change them into more usable commodities.

a. Resources
b. 6-3-5 Brainwriting
c. 180SearchAssistant
d. Power III

Chapter 1

1. b	2. d	3. a	4. d	5. b	6. d	7. d	8. d	9. b	10. a
11. d	12. d	13. d	14. a	15. a	16. b	17. c	18. c	19. d	20. a

Chapter 2

1. c	2. d	3. d	4. d	5. c	6. d	7. d	8. b	9. a	10. b
11. a	12. d	13. d	14. c	15. b	16. b	17. a	18. c		

Chapter 3

1. b	2. c	3. c	4. d	5. b	6. d	7. a	8. a	9. d	10. a
11. d	12. d	13. d	14. b	15. d	16. c	17. d	18. d	19. b	

Chapter 4

1. d	2. d	3. d	4. d	5. b	6. d	7. b	8. d	9. c	10. b
11. d	12. d	13. d	14. d	15. d	16. c	17. b	18. b	19. c	

Chapter 5

1. b	2. d	3. a	4. d	5. b	6. a	7. d	8. d	9. c	10. c
11. b	12. d	13. c							

Chapter 6

1. b	2. d	3. b	4. d	5. a	6. b	7. d	8. b	9. a	10. b
11. d	12. d	13. b	14. d	15. d	16. d	17. a			

Chapter 7

1. d	2. d	3. b	4. d	5. d

Chapter 8

1. a	2. b	3. b	4. c	5. b	6. a

Chapter 9

1. d	2. b	3. c	4. d	5. c	6. a	7. d	8. a	9. d	10. d

Chapter 10

1. a	2. c	3. c	4. d	5. c	6. d	7. c	8. b	9. c	10. a
11. d	12. d								

Chapter 11

1. b	2. d	3. d	4. a	5. d	6. c	7. b	8. a	9. d	10. d
11. c	12. d	13. c	14. c						

Chapter 12

1. d	2. d	3. a	4. c	5. d	6. c	7. d	8. c	9. a

Chapter 13

1. d	2. c	3. d	4. d	5. a	6. c	7. d	8. d	9. d	10. b
11. d	12. d	13. d	14. b	15. a					

www.ingramcontent.com/pod-product-compliance
Lightning Source LLC
Chambersburg PA
CBHW081219230426
43666CB00015B/2805
* 9 7 8 1 4 2 8 8 6 8 8 0 9 *